GRAPHOLOGY

GRAPHOLOGY

PETER WEST

ELEMENT

Shaftesbury, Dorset • Boston, Massachusetts • Melbourne, Victoria

© Element Books Limited 1999

First published in Great Britain in 1999 by
ELEMENT BOOKS LIMITED
Shaftesbury, Dorset SP7 8BP

Published in the USA in 1999 by
ELEMENT BOOKS INC.
160 North Washington Street, Boston MA 02114

Published in Australia in 1999 by
ELEMENT BOOKS
and distributed by Penguin Australia Ltd
487 Maroondah Highway, Ringwood, Victoria 3134

Designed and created with
The Bridgewater Book Company

ELEMENT BOOKS LIMITED
Managing Editor *Miranda Spicer*
Senior Commissioning Editor *Caro Ness*
Editor *Finny Fox-Davies*
Group Production Director *Clare Armstrong*
Production Manager *Susan Sutterby*
Production Controller *Linsey Denholm*

THE BRIDGEWATER BOOK COMPANY
Art Director *Terry Jeavons*
Designer *Alison Honey*
Editorial Director *Sophie Collins*
Managing Editor *Anne Townley*
Project Editor *Caroline Earle*
Picture Research *Lynda Marshall*
Endpapers *Sarah Young*

Printed and bound in Great Britain by Butler & Tanner Ltd, Frome, Somerset

British Library Cataloguing in Publication
data available

Library of Congress Cataloging in Publication data available

ISBN: 1-86204-488-0

Picture credits:
Bridgeman Art Library: 4 (Sotheby's London), 8 (Musée D'Orsay, Paris),
9 (Private Collection); Image Bank: 1, 27c, 31, 45.

CONTENTS

WHAT IS GRAPHOLOGY?

Graphology can be defined as the study and analysis of handwriting to interpret character and personality. The graphologist cannot predict the future and does not require extra sensory perception or an over-developed intuition to analyze a sample of script, but with skill and experience he or she should be able to predict a person's reactions and responses based on a page of their handwriting.

FEELINGS AND THOUGHTS

Handwriting is silent but it is a most expressive gesture of personality that should never be ignored. Moreover, handwriting also reflects the mood and emotional state of the writer at the time; these are always changing, and this is why you do not write the same way all the time. Because of this variability of our feelings and thoughts, handwriting can differ from year to year, day to day, or even hour to hour. You will discover visible evidence of the insights that handwriting provides time and time again as you study graphology.

AN EARLY 15TH-CENTURY PORTRAIT OF A NOBLEWOMAN INTENT ON HER WRITING.

WHAT DO I NEED?

The most suitable sample of handwriting for analysis should be around fifty to a hundred words in length, on a sheet of standard (A4) unlined paper and contain the author's signature. The writer should use their normal pen, not a fiber-tip; and never a pencil.

The script should be a piece of original prose and not a copy of something: a recent letter or a series of notes taken over a short period are ideal. It is best not to have anything written specifically for analysis as this will be too artificial.

JANE AUSTEN WAS AN AVID LETTER WRITER.

OSCAR WILDE AND AN EXAMPLE OF HIS WRITING.

WHEN YOU BEGIN ANALYSIS

Start at the end of the script and work back toward the beginning. This may sound unusual but it is for a good reason.

We tend to be extra careful at the start of any message, whether it is a job application or a love letter, but by the time we get near the finish we are more relaxed and write far more naturally than we did at the beginning. Once we become more involved with the actual content of our letter, we pay less attention to the manner in which we are forming the written words.

Remember that each character trait revealed in a sample of script represents only one clue to the complete personality and should never be taken in isolation or as representative of the whole character.

ELIZABETH I WAS QUEEN OF ENGLAND WHEN APPEARANCE WAS AN IMPORTANT PART OF DIPLOMACY. SHE HAD A DELIBERATELY FLORID SIGNATURE THAT WAS DESIGNED TO IMPRESS PEOPLE.

OUR WRITING AT THE END OF A
LETTER GIVES AWAY MORE ABOUT US
THAN AT THE BEGINNING.

A QUIRK OF STYLE

A quirk of style is no more than that, it is a pointer toward a particular characteristic. Further, all clues, signs, and traits can have both negative and positive aspects, and this must also be taken into account when analyzing someone's handwriting.

Observe and evaluate the whole of the handwriting sample with great care: try and learn how to balance and counterbalance all the different meanings that are conveyed by the handwriting as you find them.

QUALITY OF THE PAPER

Note the type of pen that was used, the color of the ink, and the quality of the paper, because all these factors will contribute toward a graphologist's assessment. Be sure, too, to check if the writer is left-handed for this will also have a distinct bearing on your evaluation.

Work your way steadily and carefully through the text and do not make pronouncements until entirely satisfied that you have taken account of all the nuances within the sample.

THE ORIGINS OF GRAPHOLOGY

It is clear, from a number of sources, both Eastern and Western, that handwriting has been scrutinized closely throughout history as a means of ascertaining status, character, and even temperament.

THE HISTORICAL PERSPECTIVE

Writing in 120 C.E., the historian Suetonius criticized the handwriting of Octavius Augustus Caesar, the emperor of Rome at that time. He did not like the way Caesar cramped his writing to avoid starting a new line. Suetonius was perceptive enough to draw conclusions about the emperor's personality from this.

From a different culture, an 11th-century Chinese philosopher, Kuo Jo-hsu, wrote that, "handwriting always shows whether it is written by a noble or a peasant..."

THE CELEBRATED AUTHOR EMILE ZOLA MADE REFERENCES TO GRAPHOLOGY IN HIS WRITINGS.

There are a few rare references to handwriting analysis occurring in western Europe before 1622; the year when a professor from the University of Bologna, Camillo Baldi, published the first detailed work on the subject which is the accepted origin of modern graphology. However, the term itself was not introduced until 1871 when it was coined by the Abbé Jean Hyppolyte Michon, who became known as the founding father of modern graphology.

The German philosopher, Gottfried Leibnitz, remarked in the 17th century on the connection between character and

A PORTRAIT BY THOMAS GAINSBOROUGH, WHO
USED HIS SITTERS' SCRIPTS TO GAIN A BETTER
UNDERSTANDING OF HIS SUBJECTS.

handwriting. In 1792 J. Grohman of Wittenburg wrote a treatise on handwriting analysis, prompting the great German poet, dramatist, and scientific researcher Johann Goethe to write that he believed in its accuracy. The English portrait painter Thomas Gainsborough always kept on his easel letters written by his subjects to give greater insight into them while painting their portraits. Sir Walter Scott made observations on writing and character in his novel *Chronicles of the Canongate*.

Among the many prominent writers from the 18th to the early 20th centuries who mention graphology in their writings are Baudelaire, Browning, Chekhov, Conan Doyle, Dumas, Einstein, Jung, Lavater, Lombroso, Kretzshmer, and Zola.

The first 25 years of the 20th century saw great advances in the technique of handwriting analysis in Europe, mainly in Austria, France, and Germany, and also, to a lesser degree, in North America.

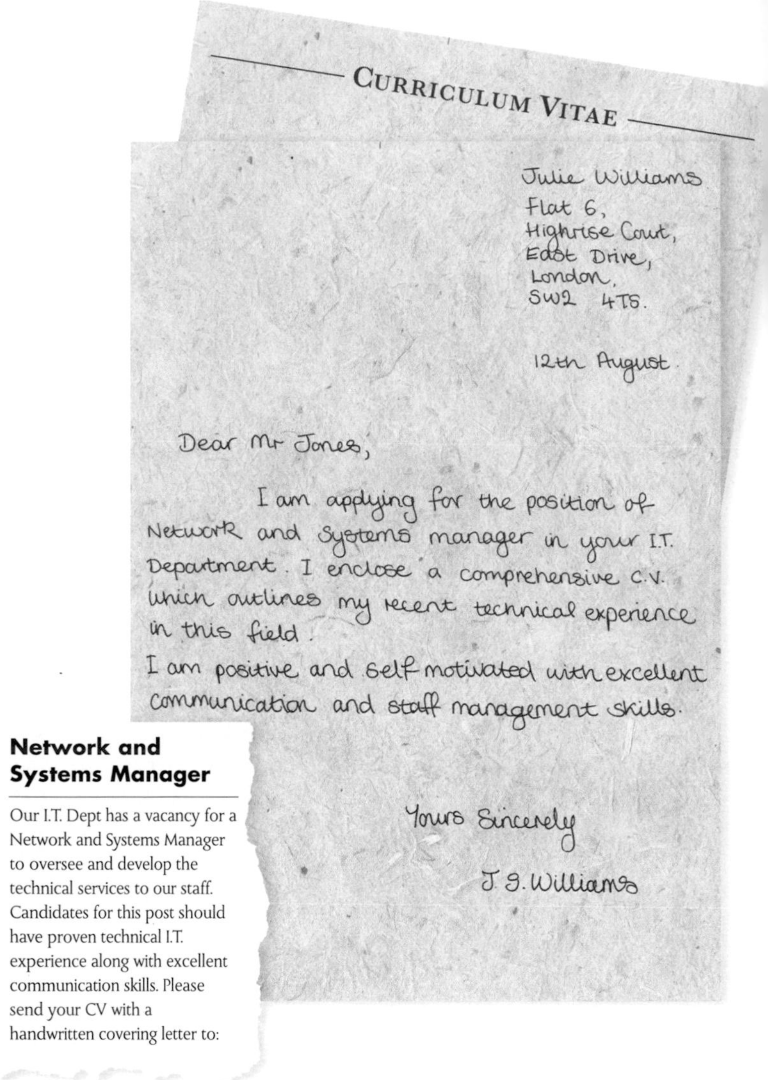

---------- CURRICULUM VITAE ----------

Julie Williams
Flat 6,
Highrise Court,
East Drive,
London,
SW2 4TS.

12th August.

Dear Mr Jones,

I am applying for the position of
Network and Systems manager in your I.T.
Department. I enclose a comprehensive C.V.
which outlines my recent technical experience
in this field.
I am positive and self motivated with excellent
communication and staff management skills.

Yours Sincerely
J.E. Williams

Network and Systems Manager

Our I.T. Dept has a vacancy for a
Network and Systems Manager
to oversee and develop the
technical services to our staff.
Candidates for this post should
have proven technical I.T.
experience along with excellent
communication skills. Please
send your CV with a
handwritten covering letter to:

GRAPHOLOGY TODAY

Graphology is now widely used as a means of personality assessment. People often go to graphologists for an assessment of their capabilities before applying for a job or to check compatibility with someone with whom they wish to have a relationship. Many employment agencies and employers ask for job applications in the applicant's own handwriting, which they can then pass on to a handwriting analyst for their assessment of the person.

The enormous strides made in assessment astonish cynics and the open-minded alike. Books have been written on the importance of the letters i and t alone; it is said that even health problems may be detected in their early stages by handwriting experts.

Graphology is now widespread. In nearly every civilized country in the world, analysts are retained as consultants or researchers. Handwriting was once described as brain writing, which means that it must also reflect character. There is only one way to find out the truth of this and that is to practice the art yourself...

BEFORE STARTING A RELATIONSHIP MANY PEOPLE OFTEN CONSULT GRAPHOLOGISTS TO CHECK THE COMPATIBILITY OF THEIR POTENTIAL PARTNER.

THE WHOLE VIEW

When first you obtain a sample of handwriting you should take in the whole view. This means looking at the way the writing is set out on the paper and the width allowed for each margin by the writer.

POINTS TO OBSERVE

Most people have good visual perception, which will be reflected in the way their script is placed on a page, but there are subtle variations that are revealing to the analyst.

• Writing of even proportion with equal margins all round shows a meticulous approach to everyday tasks and above-average intelligence.

• A wide left-hand margin shows a friendly and considerate person but with a hint of reserve in the overall personality.

• A wide right-hand margin suggests a reserved social nature. This is someone who does not mix too freely. The writer may lack spontaneity and have little confidence in their abilities.

• A wide top margin shows an indifference toward life and people in general together with a straightforward, matter-of-fact approach.

• The right-hand margin is usually uneven. There are very few people who are able to plan their handwriting well enough to maintain a neat right edge but the untidier and more uneven the margin is, the more obvious the lack of forethought in their makeup.

• An uneven left-hand margin implies a spontaneous nature. These people go with the flow of events; chameleon-like, they change color and change their coats to match their environment.

• If the left-hand margin gradually widens it suggests an impulsive or impatient nature. Money just passes

EVENLY PROPORTIONED WRITING WITH
NEAT MARGINS REVEALS A METICULOUS
AND WELL-ORDERED MIND.

Graphology can be defini
and analysis of handw
character and personalis
Graphologist cannot pr
and does not need extra
perception or an over-de
to analyze a sample
with skill and experien
should be able to pre
reactions and responses
page of their handw

through this person's hands because they have a self-indulgent streak in their nature.

- If the left-hand margin gradually becomes narrower, it suggests that the writer feels they have revealed too much and now wishes to put the brakes on. This particular personality is economical and cautious with everything, particularly money, and does not take well to being criticized or proved wrong.

- A right-hand margin that grows progressively narrower is fairly common. These writers start most things with reserve and, as familiarity increases, lose their initial reticence and become more natural.

- If the writing has little or no margins at all, you can expect two quite opposing personality traits. There is austerity, some stinginess, and an acquisitive nature but also generosity, and these people will often put their collecting nature to good use by raising money for charity.

- Wide margins found all around the paper indicate a sense of isolation. Such writers are withdrawn, not keen on social intercourse, and inwardly lonely.

Script that is illegible in places is discourteous and irksome to the reader and unrhythmic writing or poor quality lettering shows that the writer has an immature approach to life, weak organizational skills, and a lack of self-discipline. Inconsistencies in the writing, both in the style and in the execution of it, imply that there is a temporary imbalance in the nature, usually emotional. By contrast, a legible, well-written script with a pleasant cadence and balanced rhythm suggests a well-adjusted, happy, and contented personality.

A HAPPY AND WELL-BALANCED PERSONALITY WILL PRODUCE AN ATTRACTIVE AND LEGIBLE SCRIPT.

> I'm an Elder T Hoops
> We had Bible st
> Prayer and singin
> Debbie I picked
> Sandi Patti recor

SOME PEOPLE NATURALLY PRODUCE
UNEVEN AND UNPLEASANT HANDWRITING,
EVEN WITH LINES TO GUIDE THEM.

graphology report, ~ as I am very
in this subject.

As you will see from the above
Female and 40 years old. I do so
is satisfactory for your evaluation
forward to hearing from you shortl
~ Many thanks ~

NEAT HANDWRITING IS NOT ONLY
PLEASING ON THE EYE, IT SHOWS
COURTESY TO THE RECIPIENT.

HANDWRITING SLOPE

Handwriting tends to slope up or down from an imaginary horizontal baseline. The words themselves and even the individual letters often show signs of sloping, and graphologists always prefer to assess a text on unlined paper in order to study the consistency of this line slope.

INDIVIDUAL WORDS SLOPING UPWARD SUGGEST SOMEONE WITH EXCESSIVE SELF-CONFIDENCE AND A BREEZY OPTIMISM.

CHECK THE SLOPE

Handwriting often seems horizontal but each individual word usually slopes upward or downward. If handwriting slopes downward, then the author is likely to need constant assurance in order to boost a chronic lack of self-confidence. The reverse type of handwriting, where the even line is maintained by the writer but each word slopes upward, is suggestive of an over-optimistic nature, misplaced self-confidence, and lack of attention to detail.

CHECK THE BASELINE

A wavy baseline shows the writer is easily influenced by outside forces. This person is inconsistent and moody and because of incorrectly channeled energy, their talent may be wasted. If the baseline is really erratic, it reveals an indecisive, unreliable, unstable, and not always trustworthy nature. These people are easily sidetracked and welcome anything to relieve their boredom.

A horizontal baseline repeated over and over is quite rare but this reflects tight emotional control. The writer is rational, reasonable, reliable, and even-tempered, but is also usually dull and uninteresting. It can, however, suggest someone with a calculating nature.

Writing that rises upward at the end of each line is indicative of an optimistic nature. Such people are affectionate, self-confident, and not easily discouraged.

Conversely, writing that slopes downward at the end of each line is a clear sign of depression and physical tiredness. There will often be lack of enthusiasm for any current activities or projects.

Handwriting may bow upward, rise toward the middle, and then return to the baseline. This writer

WRITING IN LINES THAT SLOPE DOWN
INDICATES TIREDNESS AND DEPRESSION.

displays initial enthusiasm for a plan but quickly loses interest and often does not finish what they started.

The reverse of this, a dished or concave effect, shows the writer is initially cautious but, once a scheme is under way and doubts have evaporated they become increasingly enthusiastic and pursue it to a successful conclusion. They usually finish tasks that they have been set.

Handwriting samples that are submitted on lined notepaper displaying all of these variations can emphasize both the positive and negative aspects of these interpretations. As a general rule, people who use lined notepaper usually do so from feelings of inner insecurity. They have a need to maintain an outward feeling of confidence at all times.

WRITING THAT GOES UPWARD TOWARD THE
END OF LINES INDICATES AN AFFECTIONATE
AND SUNNY TEMPERAMENT.

SOMEONE WHOSE WRITING RISES IN THE
MIDDLE OF LINES THEN FALLS IS LIKELY TO
LACK STAYING POWER.

THE IMPORTANT WORD

One word sometimes stands out on a page, even on lined paper, because of its position either slightly higher or a little lower than the rest of the line. Should such a word be slightly higher, it implies that this word represents something of great importance to the writer. It may occur in a letter applying for a new job or promotion. When a word falls below the baseline, the writer is likely to have some uneasiness connected with the meaning of that word: it might indicate that he or she is lying or not telling the complete truth.

> hich I would like a report
> I am unable to send signa
> did this as it took me a l
> is Sample alone.

PEOPLE WHO USE LINED PAPER FOR THEIR
LETTERS ARE OFTEN INSECURE AND FEEL
THEY NEED TO LOOK CONFIDENT.

> ene not to be trusted with
> thig these days - you seen
> able to do what you ever

IF A WORD IS WRITTEN HIGHER THAN THE
OTHERS IN THE LINE, THE WRITER IS
UNCONSCIOUSLY DRAWING ATTENTION TO IT.

✶

HANDWRITING SLANT

✶

The slant of a person's handwriting is one of several outward expressions of their emotional outlook and response to other people. It shows whether the subject is reserved or impersonal, affectionate and demonstrative, or aloof and self-contained.

FORWARD OR BACKWARD?

Handwriting may be very upright, may slant forward to the right-hand side of the page, or may recline with a backward slant to the left-hand side. Degrees of this are shown opposite.

Backward- or left-slanting script usually indicates an introvert: one who holds back, doesn't trust others easily, and hides their inner feelings from everyone but the really closest of friends. This person will have few friends as a rule, but a very wide-ranging circle of acquaintants. The mask of apparent indifference will occasionally slip and you will be surprised at the depth of real emotional feeling and sensitivity this person can display.

Writing that is very reclined is rarely seen; however, such writers strive for as much independence as they can get. They are hard people to get to know and keep you at arms' length. They often have a quite charming "public" face but that is as far they will go.

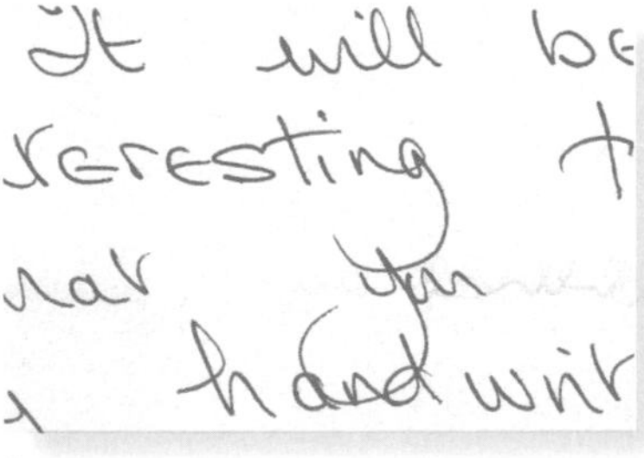

SHY AND RESERVED PEOPLE, WHO ARE DIFFICULT TO GET TO KNOW, OFTEN HAVE BACKWARD-SLANTING SCRIPTS.

I
90°
95° | 85° 80°
110°   70°
120°   60°

180°

MOST PEOPLE'S HANDWRITING SLANTS ONLY A SMALL
DEGREE AWAY FROM THE PERPENDICULAR.

Дорогой Миша!

Наступает лето, скоро будет тепло, и
чаще думаю об отдыхе. Может быть, и у нас
и у меня отпуск будет летом, и мы будем

ABOVE: THIS RUSSIAN EXAMPLE HAS A
REGULAR SLANT TO THE RIGHT, TO ABOUT
30° OFF THE PERPENDICULAR.

BELOW: THE BACKWARD SLANT IN THIS
WRITING RUNS TO AROUND 120° FROM
THE BASELINE.

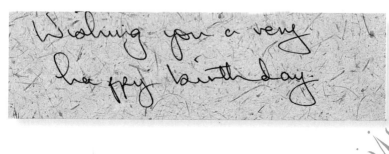

Wishing you a very
happy birthday

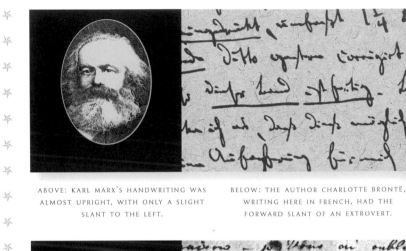

ABOVE: KARL MARX'S HANDWRITING WAS ALMOST UPRIGHT, WITH ONLY A SLIGHT SLANT TO THE LEFT.

BELOW: THE AUTHOR CHARLOTTE BRONTË, WRITING HERE IN FRENCH, HAD THE FORWARD SLANT OF AN EXTROVERT.

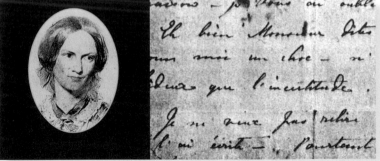

PANIC CONTROL

Vertical handwriting is very rare. Four or five degrees to either side of the vertical is generally classified as upright in handwriting analysis. This style indicates confidence, independence, and stability. These people can be relied upon in an emergency because they rarely panic, such is their self-control. They flourish in supervisory work and are well equipped to hold down positions of responsibility. They will never be really happy as part of a team because they like to be in control. These people tend to have a head-over-heart attitude which they try to maintain at all times.

ANGLE OF SLANT

The forward slant is the most natural angle for any writer to use and the most frequently found. Such writers are extrovert, warm, friendly, and responsive. They are completely natural and can express themselves easily with little or no delusions.

The more moderate the angle from the upright, the more controlled and self-reliant the nature of the author. Too much of an angle indicates an impulsive personality, someone who will be very good at bluffing their way into and out of trouble.

Mixed slant in any one sample of handwriting shows versatility, but also unpredictability and an undisciplined nature. These writers will not be able to sustain concentration for long periods, but will do well in any occupation that requires them to think on their feet.

ALTHOUGH THIS SCRIPT HAS A DOMINANT BACKWARD SLOPE, THE UPRIGHTS MIXED IN SUGGEST UNPREDICTABLE EMOTIONS.

HANDWRITING ZONES

Traditionally, the parts of letters have been classified as falling into three vertical zones: upper, middle, and lower. There are also three horizontal zones: narrow, medium, and wide. Writing may or may not be divided equally between the zones. More often than not, a person's script will emphasize one or more zones at the expense of others.

UPPER ZONE

The upper zone is concerned with the creative or imaginative impulse. Writing that emphasizes the upper zone shows an imaginative mind and an ambitious nature but if this zone is over-stressed, commonsense and practicality will be lacking. Big wide loops that reach high into this zone indicate the dreamer and idealist.

When the upper area seems almost neglected, with the ascenders so small that they are virtually non-existent, the writer is alert with a more practical approach to life, a materialist who is more concerned with day-to-day matters.

upper zone
middle zone
lower zone

THIS WRITER CONSIDERABLY EXAGGERATES THE
UPPER ZONES, INDICATING STRONG IDEALISM.

MIDDLE ZONE

The middle zone is concerned with everyday life. It represents the ego and how we relate to others and the environment. Such writers need to be with people, to impress, and be noticed; they are social butterflies and can become easily bored. They tend to live for the moment and will do anything to get away from their obligations.

mōlecular str
organismic ba

THE MIDDLE ZONES OF THIS SCRIPT ARE STRONG AND DETERMINED, UNLIKE THE ALMOST NON-EXISTENT UPPER ZONES.

If this zone is small, conversely, the author will have a love of detail and an ability to concentrate for long periods at a time.

When the other handwriting zones tend to dwarf the middle one, there may be an inferiority complex at play. Alternatively, this type of script may also indicate a tendency to work in the background; the person may be the power behind the throne.

LOWER ZONE

The lower zone is concerned with the instinctual, material, and basic appetites. Possessions are important, physical sport and outdoor pursuits are favored, and the sex drive is quite strong. Long descenders with wide loops accentuate all these attributes. Unusual or strange shaped loops may imply eccentricity.

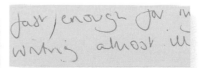

fast enough for w
writing almost ill

LOWER ZONES CAN BE EMPHASIZED WITH OR WITHOUT LOOPS. THE PRESENCE OR ABSENCE OF LOOPS IS SIGNIFICANT.

Triangular bases to loops suggest the writer is difficult to live with or awkward. Small or no loops in this zone show an independent nature. If the descenders are just downward strokes, the writer will be very determined and may have an ear for music and perhaps play an instrument. A variety of descenders in this zone (sometimes known as lower loops or "tails") implies inconsistency of approach.

BROAD, MEDIUM, OR NARROW?

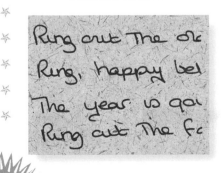

ABOVE: BROAD HANDWRITING CAN BE IDENTIFIED BY THE LETTER N HAVING A STRETCHED LOOK.

ABOVE: THE TELL-TALE FEATURE OF NARROW HANDWRITING IS A SQUEEZED LETTER N.

Handwriting may be described as either broad, medium, or narrow. As a rule, this can be assessed quite easily by looking at a sample. However, if this is not clear, look to the lower case letter n or the lower part of the letter h, particularly the hoop of the letter h. These letters can be used as indicators of the type of handwriting.

In broad handwriting, the n (or the hoop of an h) will appear oblong in shape and look slightly elongated. The medium n or the hoop of the letter h should resemble a square and the narrow n or h will have a pinched or squeezed appearance.

All broad handwriting indicates an extravagant inner nature. If it looks angular the writer will exhibit a selfish streak, however, a rounded style shows a generous nature.

Medium writing suggests a fairly placid nature, one who is reasonably content with their lot. These people are happy to let others take the lead.

Narrow handwriting indicates an inhibited and insecure type who is reserved or a little shy.

LEFT: IF THE LETTER N IS MORE OR LESS SQUARE THE HANDWRITING IS CHARACTERIZED AS BEING MEDIUM.

BROAD HANDWRITING
INDICATES AN EXTRAVAGANT
PERSON, SUCH AS SOMEONE
WHO REGARDS SHOPPING
AS A HOBBY

NARROW HANDWRITING IS
CHARACTERISTIC OF A SHY
AND INWARD-LOOKING
PERSONALITY.

PEOPLE WHO TEND TO BE
PLACID AND AT EASE WITH
LIFE WILL OFTEN HAVE
MEDIUM HANDWRITING.

HANDWRITING STYLE

There are two basic writing styles: straight (or angular), and curved (or round). Straight or angular script appears in two ways: either a straight up-and-down movement, or a thread-like style which may also appear as a curved script. Curved handwriting is either arcade, because it looks like a series of arches; or garland, like continuous shallow waves.

ANGULAR SCRIPT

Angular handwriting is an indication of strong will with a certain hardness of manner, possibly aggression, particularly in the tone of voice. The writer is rather stubborn, possibly even prejudiced and intolerant, and will brook no opposition, no matter how wrong they may be.

Threadlike script indicates a creative opportunist. At worst these people are duplicitous and insincere. They know exactly how to manipulate people and situations to get the best for themselves, while trying to make you believe that it is all for your own good.

Threadlike writing, however, can also be the result of tiredness, in which case a second or third sample should be examined. As handwriting reflects the mood and temperament of the subject at the time of writing, it may not be representative of their normal personality.

handwriting.

ANGULAR SCRIPT

Landed

THREADLIKE SCRIPT

CURVED SCRIPT

Loops are usually present with curved writing. All loops are an indication of emotion. Huge, wide upper loops suggest open and unrestrained imagination that has few limitations, but if the loops are pointed, there may be an "edge" of temper in the person's nature. Huge, wide loops in the lower zone show plenty of physical energy. The overall script level across the zones will show how well the writer controls their energy.

Arcade script shows a secretive nature, a writer who appears calm and collected on the surface but is a seething mass inside. This person doesn't like to lose face, and in extreme cases will be an obsessively controlled person, lacking spontaneity.

CURVED WRITING OFTEN HAS
LOOPS IN THE LOWER ZONE.

ARCADE SCRIPT LOOKS LIKE
A SERIES OF ARCHES ON M AND N.

GARLAND SCRIPT

Garland script reflects an impressionable emotional nature. Such a person is easy-going and rather frivolous with little thought for the future. He or she will be easily moved by sight and sound, and will be sympathetic to almost any cause presented to them.

Garlands, however, may be shallow or deep. Shallow garlands imply little depth to the character. The author of this type of script is easily led, has poor self-control, and little direction. Handwriting with deep garlands shows someone who prefers to cling to others, to an ideal or a group. Such a person is highly emotional in every respect. They may be an avid collector, or simply be reluctant to throw anything away on the basis that it might prove useful in the future.

A SHALLOW GARLAND SCRIPT (LIKE A SERIES OF SMALL WAVES) SUGGESTS SOMEONE LACKING DEPTH.

THE LARGE WAVES OF DEEP GARLANDS INDICATE AN EMOTIONAL, CLINGING PERSONALITY.

CONFUSION

A mixture or accentuation of each type occasionally appears in one script. Look for clues in what is written to see in which direction the writer is presently inclined. Heavy arcades are often written by those in the public eye, while politicians tend to use thread-like arcades. Do not be deceived but remember also that an accentuated garland script is often seen immediately after an emotional upheaval.

SPACING

Spacing between letters, words, and lines may seem unimportant but it reveals useful information about the social adaptability of the writer.

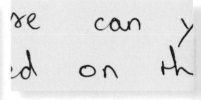

NARROW WORD SPACING (LEFT) AND AN
EXAMPLE (ABOVE) OF WIDE SPACING.

CHECKING THE SPACING

Even spacing indicates good organizational ability; muddled or cramped script implies an introvert nature plus great impulsiveness and a reliance on others; wide spacing usually suggests an extrovert personality.

Writers who allow only narrow spacing between words are rarely happy on their own. Yet although they prefer to be with other people, they are selfish and take more from a relationship than they are prepared to offer.

Wide spacing between words suggests the writer is objective and discriminating. These people prize their privacy and guard it closely. Although they seem to have a wide circle of friends, they are kept at arm's length and are really no more than acquaintances.

Irregular spacing between words suggests immaturity. It may also indicate a certain emotional instability when the sample was written.

UNEVEN SPACING BETWEEN LETTERS
AND WORDS IS A SIGN THAT THE
WRITER MAY BEHAVE ERRATICALLY.

CHECKLIST

Spacing between the lines shows how the writer relates to their environment.

• Narrow spaces suggest good inner harmony, a conscientious and careful person who is always considerate to (and of) others.

• Wide spacing implies someone unhappy within themselves. This may stem from some earlier emotional upset that the writer can never quite forget.

• Irregular spacing between lines indicates someone who is prone to erratic or undisciplined behavior.

• Very wide spacing between lines can mean a troubled emotional state. Such people can be their own worst enemy for they need help to overcome their problems but may fail to recognize this.

• Finally, irregular spacing between letters within a word implies a moody nature; one can never be quite sure what the writer may or may not do next.

NARROW LINE SPACING IS A SIGN OF A
PEACEFUL AND CONSIDERATE PERSON.

WIDE SPACING BETWEEN LINES IS
CHARACTERISTIC OF AN UNHAPPY PERSON.

CAPITAL LETTERS

Strictly speaking, a capital letter begins a word or sentence, although on rare occasions a writer may use one in the middle of a word. Capital letters – especially those in odd places – indicate the writer's ego, self-confidence, and attitude toward authority.

TRYING TO IMPRESS

The larger the letter, the greater the writer's self-esteem; the more ornate the letter is, the more flamboyant the character and the greater their need to assert their personality to impress others.

When a stroke supports a capital from the left, there is an added sense of self-importance. If this extra stroke should originate from the middle zone or below the baseline, it shows pride in appearance and vanity. An extra support stroke from the upper zone suggests the writer values achievement.

Large wide capitals imply expansiveness. If they are also ornate,

expect to find conceit and a pushy or even vulgar nature. Ambition and pride will also be present.

A STROKE SUPPORTING A CAPITAL LETTER FROM THE LOWER ZONE.

DRAMATIC OR AGGRESSIVE?

A capital written in such a way as to encircle the word suggests a patronizing and overly dramatic personality. Emphasized loops in the middle zone indicate selfishness; from the lower zone, considerable sensuality and poor taste.

A capital letter that rises from the lower zone high into the upper zone implies an aggressive, fussy, and self-opinionated type, whereas small letters are an indication of modesty or even humility.

On those rare occasions when a capital letter appears in the middle of a word, the writer is revealing an unsettled nature at the time of writing. He or she will have been emotionally disturbed in some way when the message was composed.

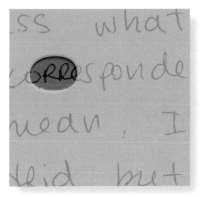

CAPITAL LETTERS IN THE MIDDLE OF
A WORD INDICATE DISTURBANCE.

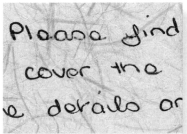

SMALL CAPITAL LETTERS ARE THE SIGN
OF A MODEST PERSON.

UNEVEN, BADLY FORMED WRITING CAN BE
ANOTHER SIGN OF EMOTIONAL DISTURBANCE.

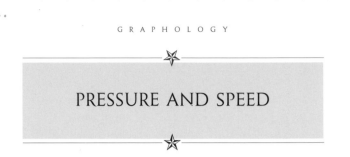

PRESSURE AND SPEED

A graphologist will assess the mood and emotional intensity of a writer from the pressure they exert in their handwriting.

HOW MUCH PRESSURE?

Pressure may be obvious in the script or can be seen or even physically felt on the reverse of the paper. In these days of the ball point pen, it is more often felt than seen.

Heavy pressure shows a strong libido, determination, enthusiasm, and resistance. It also shows that the writer is currently enjoying good health and denotes a well-balanced, confident personality.

Light pressure may be due to temporary tiredness or it may be a sign of sensitivity and flexibility. Such handwriting often suggests an intuitive or perceptive nature, but it may also mean that the willpower is poor and that the writer is an over-tolerant, easy-going, and yielding type.

Uneven pressure indicates poor personal control. This writer is changeable and may be stressed. Check the script for clues as to what is troubling them; this may reveal itself through an emphasis on certain words.

HOW MUCH SPEED?

Fast handwriting shows an alert, perceptive mind and is often evident by the enthusiasm in what is written. This spontaneous approach is usually shown by right-hand sloping script with the t bars and i dots placed well to the right.

Slow handwriting denotes an emotionally controlled character, not overly moody. This writer is inclined to be steady and consistent – possibly a little reserved or unsure.

Heavy pressure indicates confidence and determination

Ball point pens leave evidence of pressure on the back of the paper

Fast, enthusiastic handwriting denotes a perceptive mind

Dear Sue
Off on holiday
tomorrow. I can't wait!
Some sun at last!!
Julie

THE PRESSURE AND SPEED
OF HANDWRITING ALSO
GIVE CLUES TO THE
WRITER'S PERSONALITY.

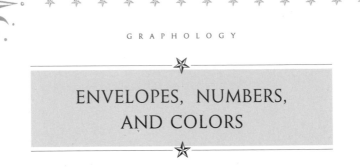

ENVELOPES, NUMBERS, AND COLORS

When we receive a letter, the first thing we look at is the handwriting on the envelope, especially if it is unfamiliar. What we should then do is observe how the address is actually written on the envelope, for that can be very revealing.

ENVELOPES

If the writing is larger than that of the letter inside, then it is likely that the author is trying to build up their personal image with you. When smaller, they are applying false modesty and are more confident than they would like you to know.

An illegible address is plain bad manners, while ostentatious writing is not far short of discourtesy. Unnecessary underlining is a pointless exercise, and someone who indulges in it may be unable to distinguish between right and wrong, and be obstinate or awkward.

An address that is placed rather too high on an envelope reveals a

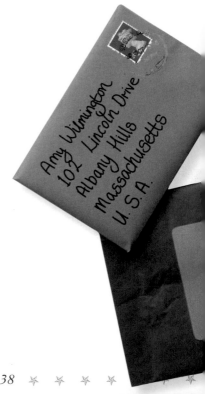

Amy Wilmington
102 Lincoln Drive
Albany Hills
Massachusetts
U. S. A.

dreamer who is careless and impractical. When placed low, expect to find a pessimist or a materialist with an acquisitive nature.

If the address is placed toward the top left, it implies an enquiring mind but a lack of confidence. Placed toward the top right it suggests carelessness or a liking for independence coupled with little regard for the conventional.

When the address is placed in the bottom left corner of the envelope, it shows a materialist with a cautious nature and an element of reserve. If put in the bottom right-hand corner, the writer is down to earth with very few illusions.

The traditional, stepped address shows an unsure and conventional type who should not be hurried into making decisions.

Annette Ourat
42, Ve du Parc
Granville

thias Koehler
68

A GREAT DEAL CAN BE
LEARNED FROM WHERE
A LETTER-WRITER PLACES
THE ADDRESS ON THE
ENVELOPE, AND THE WAY
IN WHICH IT IS WRITTEN.

NUMBERS

Numbers are an outward expression of the writer's concern with material matters: their social position and, especially, their handling of money. For a graphologist, the way that numerals are written provides very telling information about the writer's ability to manage finance.

Numbers should be evenly written and well constructed with few or no embellishments. This shows reliability. The writer will be good with money and is basically honest. If you see poorly formed numerals, it implies difficulty with money, and you would be well advised not to allow the person to handle anything but their own cash for they are prone to make mistakes through simple carelessness.

Numbers that are both badly formed and written with heavy pressure have been penned by a materialistic and/or impractical person especially if cash is involved.

A series of numbers written with colons between them instead of a comma or period indicates a reluctance to spend money on anything, even when it belongs to someone other than the writer.

Any number that has been touched up or embellished in any way suggests either uncertainty or anxiety in the writer's nature. If embellishments are found in a text which has been written slowly and using heavy pressure, keep the writer as far away from money as possible for they are just plain careless or unthinking.

Small, square-looking, and concise numerals are frequently found where the writer is skillful in technical matters. When numbers are smaller than the actual accompanying script, the writer is very likely to be involved with scientific matters in some way.

COLORS

Normally, we all choose and use the same color ink for our day-to-day written communications because, although we may not realize it, the ink we use regularly reflects our normal emotional state. This does not preclude the fact that we may pick up a pen with black, red, or any other color ink to dash off a quick note even though we might use blue as a rule.

Dark colors are associated with a passive response, where the writer's

nature is more direct and controlled. Light colors suggest that the writer is free of hang-ups, active, motivated, and energetic.

Most people use a variation of blue ink as their personal choice. Dark blue is widely used by those people who care for others. Pale blue is favored by people in creative pursuits, especially women.

Brown ink is used by naturally cautious writers who will not make a move unless they first check and recheck everything.

Green ink signifies emotional immaturity or someone who needs to be different, an individualist.

Red ink shows a love of being different or perhaps the writer is in authority and needs to be noticed. It might also be used by people who like to shock, or have some imbalance in their natures.

The use of violet ink always denotes a submissive and immature approach to life – especially among men. Women who use violet ink tend to be social butterflies.

Black ink is always used by those who must be clearly understood at all times. These writers don't just ask or state, they impose their will and are often extremely intolerant of the opinions of others.

THE CHOICE OF INK COLOR IS A SIGN OF THE CONFIDENCE AND MATURITY OF THE WRITER.

Chris Williams
flat 6,
Highrise Court,
East Drive,
London,
SW2 4TS.

Chris Williams
flat 6,
Highrise Court,
East Drive,
London,
SW2 4TS.

Williams
Flat 6,
Highrise Court,
East Drive,
London,
SW2 4TS.

Chris Williams
flat 6,
Highrise Court,
East Drive,
London,
SW2 4TS.

THE MOST POPULAR INK COLOR IS BLUE; OTHERS MAY INDICATE WEAKNESS OR INDIVIDUALITY.

REVEALING LETTERS

Certain individual letters are strong indications of personality traits in the writer. A graphologist will examine these specific letters for further clues as to how well developed those traits may be.

CHARACTER CLUES

The letters a and o will always give strong indications of character. Both these letters are closed letters, like the middle section of the letters d and g. When the top part of these ovals is not quite closed, the nature is open and sociable but inclined to be chatty. If the tops are wide open, the person will tend to gossip. If these ovals are left open at the baseline, it might be unwise to trust the penmanship for it indicates a degree of hypocrisy

THE LETTERS A AND O ARE PROPERLY CLOSED LETTERS, BUT SOME PEOPLE LEAVE A GAP AT THE TOP OR BOTTOM.

and the tendency for the writer to be not always what they seem.

Narrow middle zone sections indicate conservatism and secrecy, and wide ovals show tolerance and fair-mindedness. If writers make loops inside ovals, it indicates that they are discreet but at the same time are unable to be really honest with themselves.

Ovals that look like strokes suggest the writer has a manipulative and indirect nature which may not mean to deceive but invariably does so through insincerity. A knot found on the top of an oval letter could indicate that they employ a certain amount of deception in their dealings with other people.

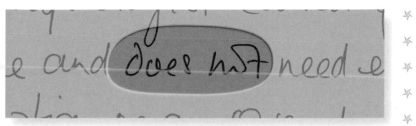

IF CLOSED LETTERS ARE LEFT OPEN AT THEIR TOPS, THIS IS A SIGN THAT THE
WRITER HAS A FRIENDLY AND CHATTY PERSONALITY. IF THEY ARE OPEN AT THE
BOTTOM THE WRITER MAY NOT BE TRUSTWORTHY.

LOOPS FOR EMOTION

A loop in any script always signifies emotion, so loops in letters that should not have one, such as d or t, show a highly developed emotional personality; the writer will often be overly sensitive with a dislike of criticism, no matter how justified it may be.

On the other hand, if letters that should be looped, such as a, b, f, g, h, j, k, l, p, q, and y, are made with a stroke instead, the author is someone who likes to take action, prefers the direct approach to problems, and who keeps any emotion well under control.

If a cross formation appears anywhere, in a loop or otherwise, a certain amount of inner unhappiness or depression will be present and the writer may be resigned to the fact that they feel low.

AN UNNECESSARY LOOP MAY BE GIVEN TO THE LETTER D (ABOVE LEFT), WHILE SOME
WRITERS MAKE THE LOOPS IN LETTERS THAT SHOULD HAVE THEM, SUCH AS G,
EXTREMELY LARGE AND PRONOUNCED (ABOVE RIGHT).

LETTERS WRITTEN ON A STRAIGHT BASELINE AS IF
ON A RULER INDICATE SOMEONE WHO IS
RELUCTANT TO ADMIT TO MISTAKES.

THICK AND THIN

Individual letters made with thick strokes suggest a creative personality, one who responds readily to light, dark, sound, and color. Impressionable, sentimental, and easily wounded by a wrong word, this writer will become completely absorbed in the matter at hand to the exclusion of all else.

When individual letters are written with thin strokes, the writer is usually reserved or restrained and unable to express his or her feelings properly. They may be refined but also feel they must conform rigidly to social protocols and can seem cold by nature as a consequence.

Sometimes individual letters appear so fixed and straight that it looks as if they were written with a ruler underneath. This denotes a writer who does not like to be seen to make mistakes, who will admit to errors but does not actually wish to reveal them. Such people are often unable to relax in company, particularly being awkward with any public displays of affection such as those small emotional touches between close couples.

LOOPS AND STROKES

Thick and thin strokes found in the same word and odd unnecessary loops mean the writer has a moody and changeable nature. They can be stirred easily one way or the other, though not necessarily as expected. Such people are consequently highly unpredictable.

The letter i can be particularly revealing, especially in the way the dot is produced. An i with a high-flying dot shows imagination and ambition, but a low-placed dot shows concentration and a more precise nature. No dot at all suggests carelessness or absent-mindedness, but if the dot is joined to the following letter, it suggests a swift, perceptive mind. A circle over the letter i instead of a dot always indicates a person who must "feel" different from everyone else. This is someone who makes a conscious effort to stand out from the crowd, and is probably faddish in dress, gesture, and diet.

CIRCLES INSTEAD OF DOTS OVER THE LETTER I ARE WRITTEN BY PEOPLE WHO WANT TO APPEAR DIFFERENT, OFTEN BEING FADDISH IN FOOD AND CLOTHES.

✯

FIRST AND LAST LETTERS

✯

If you wish to know more about how sociable the writer is, in examining the letter shapes pay close attention to the way they write both the first letter of a written word and the final one.

FIRST LETTER

The first letter of a written word shows the general confidence and social openness of the personality. It also shows if the writer is shy or impulsive, has a sense of responsibility, or just muddles through life.

Introductory strokes to a letter or word reveal how quickly, if at all, the writer adjusts to new people in their social circle, and how they react to fresh situations in general.

Almost any additional starting stroke to a letter shows concern with detail, but if the stroke is a long one, then the writer may be finicky and over-fussy. If the stroke comes from the lower zone, the writer is self-defensive and/or self-protective and

INTRODUCTORY STROKES TO LETTERS, AS SHOWN ON THE LETTER M HERE, INDICATE HOW THE WRITER ADJUSTS TO NEW PEOPLE.

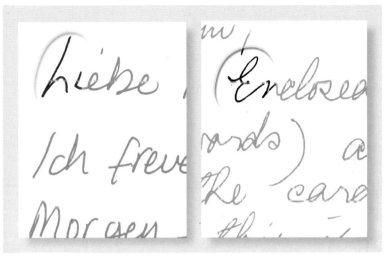

AN INITIAL LETTER SEPARATED FROM
ITS WORD INDICATES GOOD
INTUITIVE SKILLS.

AN INITIAL LETTER JOINED TO THE
WORD SHOWS THE WRITER IS
METHODICAL.

has a tendency to shun or avoid personal responsibility.

If the letter is large with an extended triangular base, expect a strong degree of vanity in the make-up of this person. Any angular extension like this also adds a materialistic streak.

An upper zone extension in the form of a loop shows a dreamer who never really understands precisely what is expected of them. Consequently, this person will always bluff their way through every situation.

If the first part of an initial letter rises, it suggests a lack of confidence: the writer may be slightly diffident. Conversely, when the first part of the letter descends, expect to find some arrogance in the nature and not a little selfishness.

Separated initial letters that stand away from the rest of the word show intuition, someone always prepared to play a hunch. If, however, a letter is joined to the rest of the word, it means that details are worked out in advance – little margin is left for error.

FORGED MANUSCRIPT AND COPY OF SIGNATURE

ACTUAL SIGNATURE

THE INFAMOUS WILLIAM HENRY IRELAND (1775–1835) PRODUCED COUNTLESS FORGERIES OF SHAKESPEARE AND OTHER ELIZABETHAN WRITERS. ABOVE IS HIS FORGERY OF THE FIRST PAGE OF *KING LEAR* — COMPARE THIS WITH SHAKESPEARE'S ACTUAL SIGNATURE BENEATH. SLOWLY PRODUCED FINAL STROKES CAN INDICATE FORGERY.

LAST LETTERS

The final letter of any word, especially at the end of a sentence or a line, indicates three things: the level of attention of the writer, their mood, and sociability and the speed of writing. The latter is most important because in assessing the speed of the script, the graphologist can also assess the degree of spontaneity with which the writer has worked.

In cases where there are no ending strokes the writer is direct, possibly even abrupt with people. A final stroke that swings upward to the right shows activity and drive, but if it swings downward and to the right, the writer has a generous and outgoing nature. A final stroke that curves

ABOVE: ENERGETIC, ACTIVE PEOPLE WRITE WITH A RISING FINAL STROKE.

up and over the top of the word to the left shows a self-defensive nature; if it sweeps down under the word to the left, expect materialism and a poor social mixer.

Hooks and ticks are signs of acquisition. Writers who use these are possessive and contentious people who are rarely able to achieve lasting inner satisfaction.

A diminishing final letter indicates diplomacy, maturity, and tact, while a letter that increases in size suggests naiveté, an open and frank, sometimes childlike, nature.

Considerable care must be taken when assessing these final letters because regular scriptwriting or pressure merely attests to the level of concentration; clear, even handwriting with properly formed natural endings simply indicates good personal control.

Speed suggests spontaneity, however; the act of writing is entirely natural for the writer. It is in assessing the speed of a piece of script, therefore, particularly the last letters, that the graphologist is able to look for duplicity or even forgery. No impulse is so difficult to control as one that requires constant stopping and restarting, and this is precisely what we do when we attempt to copy a style or signature; we stop at the end of a word before going on to the next one.

SIGNATURES

The main sample of a script provides details of a person's physical, intellectual, and emotional state at the time of writing (the inner person), but the signature shows the manner in which he or she wishes to be perceived by others (the outer image).

TWO SIGNATURES

Often, people have two quite different signatures, one for formal business matters, and the other for more private or intimate communications. For this reason a graphologist will always find it wiser not to value too highly a signature on its own without a further sample. One can learn much from a single example but it is not really a practical exercise.

A large, bold signature denotes a confident nature, someone who is self-assured with good leadership abilities. If a signature is larger than the body of the letter, the writer wants to be recognized and is calling for more attention. He or she is proud and ambitious with plenty of personal self-esteem.

However, if it is disproportion-ately larger than the rest of the letter, the writer will be overly proud, false, and pretentious.

When the signature is smaller than that of the body of the letter, the writer is over-sensitive and introverted, and may in an extreme case also be scheming, hypocritical, and self-protective.

Small, insignificant signatures reveal self-consciousness and a lack of confidence. These signatures are formed by people who tend to undervalue themselves. They neither ask nor seek recognition but do need a pat on the back to keep them going.

The evenly balanced signature, with lettering about the same size as the rest of the communication, shows a quietly confident nature one you cannot always ignore.

TOP: THE BOLD SIGNATURE AND SCRIPT OF THE NOVELIST DOSTOEVSKY.

ABOVE: NAPOLEON'S SIGNATURE WAS LARGER THAN HIS SCRIPT.

OPPOSITE: CHARLES DICKENS HAD AN ELABORATE SIGNATURE FOR PUBLIC AND FORMAL DOCUMENTS.

CAN YOU READ IT?

The legibility of a signature also gives important information about temperament. A legible signature shows a writer is reasonably outgoing and discriminating and dislikes unnecessary fuss. An unreadable signature with a legible text is a sign of impatience. This suggests the writer has something to hide and may not always be trustworthy.

An illegible signature with equally illegible text is plain bad manners. They care little for you or your opinion, are selfish, basically insecure, and thoughtless.

ABOVE: WILLIAM SHAKESPEARE'S SIGNATURE ON HIS LAST WILL AND TESTAMENT. THE WRITING VARIES THROUGHOUT THE WILL.

BELOW: THE POET BYRON'S SIGNATURE MATCHES HIS SCRIPT, ALBEIT WITH A FINAL DRAMATIC FLOURISH.

WHERE IS IT?

A signature placed to the left of the page could suggest that the writer has a lack of confidence and is generally someone who clings to the past, but it may also be a response to a traditional method of teaching letter-writing.

When the signature is placed to the right of the page, a self-confident and easy-going nature is evident; the writer will be sociable and gregarious. If, however, a writer signs their name in the middle of the page, it suggests a need for personal recognition, or to be in the center of whatever is going on.

Look closely at the space between the text and the signature. If the signature is close to the last line, it indicates a belief in what is written but one with a wide space between it and the last line can mean the writer is not being entirely truthful.

Watch out, too, for discrepancies between the slope of the text and the slope of the signature. If the main text slopes forward but the signature slopes to the left or is upright, the writer is literally applying the brakes. There is little or no spontaneity and emotions are on a tight rein. However, text that slopes to the left with a forward-sloping signature is a sign the writer may appear warm and friendly, but in reality is cold, almost ruthless, and will allow very little to stand in their way.

BEETHOVEN'S SIGNATURE IS CLOSE TO THE LAST LINE IN THIS LETTER, SHOWING THAT HE WAS HONEST IN WHAT HE WROTE.

✵
CONCLUSION
✵

You now have a good working knowledge of basic graphology. Hopefully you will be familiar with the many clues that can help you consider the numerous and varied personality traits that lurk within every piece of handwriting from a whole document down to just a single letter.

PRACTICE MAKES PERFECT

When you assess handwriting remember that it must be the writer's normal hand and not specially written for the occasion.

Allow what you see to guide you. Each handwriting sample with its nuances and foibles will lead you to the right conclusions every time. Remember that a single piece of handwriting will reveal all our strengths and weaknesses but learning to detect them and become an expert takes time. Practice makes perfect. With practice you will find that a great deal can be learned about a person merely from a sample of their script. This may be invaluable to you when pursuing a job or seeking a suitable employee,

it can be useful in your personal relationships, or may simply turn out to be an enjoyable hobby.

Julie Williams
Flat 6,
Highrise Court,
Edge Drive,
London,
SW2 4TS.

12th August

Dear Mr Jones,

I am applying for the position of Network and Systems manager in your IT Department. I enclose a comprehensive C.V. which outlines my recent technical experience in this field.
I am positive a ...tivated with excellent
communication ...skills.

Herrn Matthias Kaehler
Pflügerstr. 68
Böblingen

USEFUL ADDRESSES

Handwriting analysis offers a variety of areas for research according to individual needs; some readers may wish to investigate the subject more fully.

The addresses of the few organizations that exist may change. Readers should apply to their local public library for current information. This may also reveal local study groups, whether independent or affiliated to main societies.

THE BRITISH INSTITUTE OF
GRAPHOLOGISTS
4th Floor, Bell Court House,
11 Blomfield Street,
London EC2M 7AY, England.

THE GRAPHOLOGY SOCIETY
33 Bonningtons, Thriftwood,
Hutton, Brentwood,
Essex CM13 2TL, England.

THE ACADEMY OF
GRAPHOLOGY
1 Queens Elm Square,
London SW3 6ED, England.

KNOWLEDGE OF GRAPHOLOGY CAN
BOTH BE OF PRACTICAL BENEFIT AND
PROVIDE AN ENJOYABLE HOBBY.

THE SOCIETY FOR THE STUDY OF
PHYSIOLOGICAL PATTERNS
39 Larchwood House,
Baywood Square, Chigwell,
Essex IG7 HAY, England
(The SSPP correlates findings on astrology, chirology, graphology, numerology, and phrenology.)

THE ASSOCIATION FOR
GRAPHOLOGICAL STUDIES
665 San Rodolfo Drive, Suite 124,
Solana Beach, CA 92075, USA.

FURTHER READING

BRANSTON, Barry, *The Elements of Graphology* (Element Books 1995)

HILL, Barbara, *Graphology* (Robert Hale 1981)

HOLMES, Derek, *Stars In Their Own Write* (Robson Books 1989)

MENDEL, Alfred, *Personality in Handwriting* (Stephen Daye Press 1982)

SINGER, Eric, *Manual of Graphology* (Gerald Duckworth 1969)

WEST, Peter, *You And Your Handwriting* (Allison & Busby 1991)

INDEX